BASKETWEAVING
FOR BEGINNERS

First published in Great Britain 2019 by Search Press Limited
Wellwood, North Farm Road, Tunbridge Wells, Kent TN2 3DR

Original French title:
Vannerie créative © 2016 Groupe Eyrolles, Paris, France

English translation by Paul Carslake

Design and layout: Sophie Charbonnel

Photography: icnico – pages 8, 10, 26–27, 28, 30 bottom left, 31, 35,
37 bottom right, 39, 43, 45, 47, 48, 51, 53, 54, 55, 59, 61 bottom left,
61 right, 63, 67, 69 bottom right, 70, 73, 75 right, 77, 79 right, 81, 83,
84, 85, 87 right, 88, 91, 95, 97 right, 99, 102, 105, 107 right, 109, 112,
113, 115 right, 116, 117, 119 bottom right, 121, 125, 127 right, and
cover images.

The step-by-step photographs and the photograph on page 128 are
those of the author.

ISBN 978-1-78221-700-8

Suppliers
If you have difficulty in obtaining any of the materials and equipment
mentioned in this book, then please visit the Search Press website for
details of suppliers: www.searchpress.com

BASKETWEAVING
FOR BEGINNERS

Sylvie **Bégot**

SEARCH PRESS

CONTENTS

PROJECTS 26

ESSENTIAL RULES
& ADVICE

WORKING RULES

To create basketwork with an even and harmonious weave, you will need to follow just a few essential rules.

- The thickness of stakes and weavers: the stakes (the vertical supports) must always be thicker in diameter than the weavers. If you don't have sufficiently thick cane for the stakes, you can simply double them up.
- The relative position of stakes and weavers: as the weavers run in and out through the stakes, the stakes must remain completely straight.
- Making it sufficiently rigid: you will need spaces of just 2–3cm (¾–1¼in) between each stake to ensure that your basketry keeps its shape

STORING CANE AND SOAKING TIMES

Cane is supplied in either a 500g (17¾oz) bundle of long rods (which needs quite a bit of space for storage) or a continuous roll, in 500g (17¾oz) or 250g (8¾oz) weights; a roll is more compact for storage (and I recommend this option). Store your cane in a well-ventilated space, and away from direct light – especially for coloured cane. Any cane that you soak but do not use should be left to dry out thoroughly before storage: cane can very quickly pick up mould.

Cane soaking times

Soak your cane in a place where there is no risk of water damage to floors or walls. Despite its great flexibility, cane must always be dampened before it is worked. Ideally use warm water, as this will shorten the soaking time required.

Soaking times depend on the thickness of the cane:

- 1.5mm (¹⁄₁₆in) to 3mm (⅛in): three minutes;
- 3.5mm (⅛in) to 6mm (¼in): five minutes;
- 6.5mm (¼in) to 10mm (⅝in): ten minutes.

YOUR WORKING POSITION

You can work either at a table or kneeling down, using a cloth or apron to protect your clothes.

For right-handed basket weavers, your right hand will guide the weavers in and out of the stakes, pulling them gently into place, while the left hand, with fingers spread out like a comb, will push the weavers down to avoid leaving any 'holes' in the weave. For left-handers, it's the reverse, of course.

VARNISHES

Varnishing your basketry will give it a longer life and make it slightly more rigid.

- Apply varnish outdoors, or in a well-ventilated space.
- Remember to use acrylic varnish for any basketwork that comes into contact with food – including food for our feathered friends on the bird feeder (see pages 90–93).

GLOSSARY

Adding a weaver: place the new weaver behind the stake in the next available gap.

Adding lapping cane: position the new cane over the end of the previous one, and behind a stake: the two canes should overlap by 6cm (2¼in).

Base sticks: thick cane rods forming the basket base – connected with several rounds of weave – which will become the base of the basket.

Bodkin: a sharp metal point, fitted into a handle, used for pushing rod ends into the weave.

Border: the finishing edge of the basketwork, usually made by interlinking the stakes.

Centre cane: cane with the outer skin taken off. Generally of a matt finish.

Cross pieces: on an oval slath base (see page 15), these are the shorter sticks that are pierced, allowing the longer base sticks to run through them.

Fitching: a form of siding which leaves the stakes exposed without weave, or in a crossed-over pattern.

Flat band cane: centre cane with a flat profile on each side.

Flat-oval profile: cane that is flat on one side, oval on the other.

Glossy lapping cane: made from the bark of the rattan plant, which gives it the glossy outer side.

God's Eye: a form of decorative binding.

Interval: the space between two stakes.

Lapping cane: a form of centre cane with a flat-oval profile.

Liner: a rod inserted alongside a stake for decoration or strength.

Long sticks: the sticks that follow the length of an oval base.

Packing: making shorter rows of weave to fill awkwardly shaped gaps.

Pairing: a weaving stroke using two rods.

Pricking up: pushing the stakes into a vertical position.

Randing: a weaving stroke using one rod.

Rib: the rod used as the stake in a round basket.

Rod: a length of cane used either for weaving or for the stakes.

Siding: the vertical section of the basketweave.

Slath: the rigid structure made from the base sticks.

Slewing: a weaving stroke using two or more rods that do not cross each other.

Spokes: alternative name for the base sticks and the stakes when working from a round base.

Stakes: vertical rods that form the frame of the basketwork siding. Also known as spokes when working a round basket.

Sticks: short lengths of rod forming the base.

Stroke: a weaving style, such as pairing or randing.

Triple weave: a type of waling weave using three rods.

Upsett: weaving one round using a waling weave of three or four rods. It provides strength and rigidity.

Waling weave: weave using three or more rods (*see also* triple weave).

Weaver: any rod that is used for weaving.

Note: For the projects in this book, 'cane' refers to round profile centre cane – e.g. 2mm (¹∕₁₆in) undyed cane is centre cane, 2mm (¹∕₁₆in) diameter, in undyed colour.

'Lapping cane' refers to flat-oval centre cane, typically around 5mm (¼in) wide.

TECHNIQUES

BASES

Round slath base

Base
This is a rigid base, and will require eight base sticks.

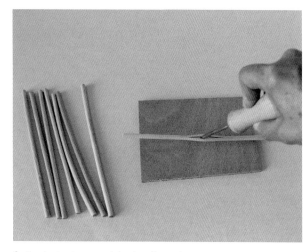

1. Soak the base sticks for five minutes in warm water. Use a pencil to mark the mid-point of four of the sticks, and then pierce each one using a bodkin over a hard surface.

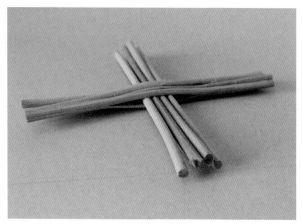

2. Insert each of the four other sticks through the pierced sticks to create a cross. Adjust them so that the arms of the cross are even.

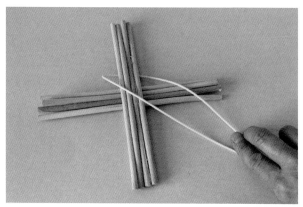

3. Soak one long weaver of 1.5mm or 2mm (¹⁄₁₆in) diameter. Fold it in half, and twist it at the fold to prevent it snapping. Place the weaver around the four base sticks.

4. Start a pairing weave (see page 18).

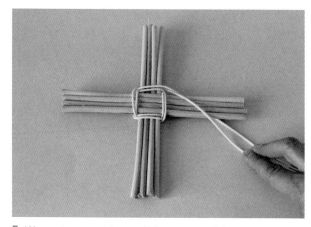

5. Weave two rounds on all four arms of the cross.

6. For the third round, divide each set of sticks into two spokes.

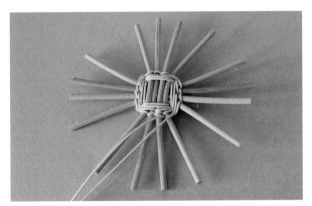

7. For the fourth round, separate all the spokes as regularly as possible, and weave around the whole base.

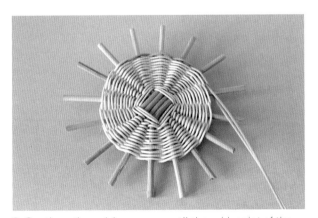

8. Continue the pairing weave until the mid-point of the spokes, then change to a wider weaver – one weaver at 2.5mm (³⁄₃₂in) and then 3mm (¹⁄₈in) – if the base is more than 20cm (7¾in) across.

9. Finish the base by securing the weavers. Fold over and insert the ends into the weave.

Inserting stakes (or 'spokes')

1. Trim the base sticks level with the outside edge.

2. Insert the stakes either side of each base stick.

Making the upsett

The upsett will be made from just one round of four-rod 'waling' weave. It holds the side stakes in place and keeps them evenly spaced; it also provides a more stable base for the basket.

1. Cut four rods, each measuring 15cm (6in) longer than the circumference of the base.

2. Position the base with the new rods opposite you, placing one in each space.

3. Hold them in place with a clothes peg, and weave them in as follows: in front of three stakes, behind one stake, and out to the front. Start with the rod furthest to your left – the red rod in the photograph.

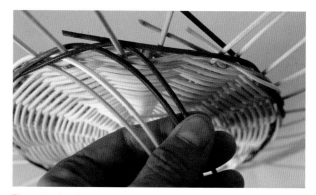

The red rod ends up going through the same space as it started.

4. The rod must finish at the exact same place that it started.

5. Now weave the next rod (green) in the same way, above the previous one, and then the other two.

6. The rod ends are all tucked in place against a spoke. The upsett is complete.

Oval slath base

The oval slath base is made up of long base sticks and shorter cross sticks.

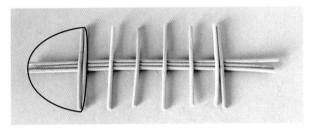

1. Cut the three long sticks and the eight cross sticks. Thread the long sticks through the pierced cross sticks, and arrange them all evenly, with four singles and a pair at each end. The length of the remaining long sticks is roughly the radius of a semi-circle, as shown above.

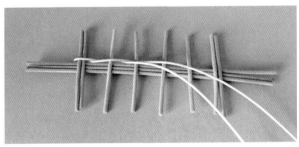

2. As with the round base, fold a long weaver in two on one of the double cross-pieces, and start the pairing weave (see page 18).

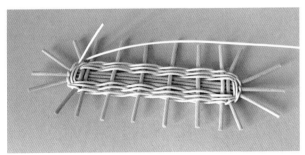

3. Weave two rounds pairing. On the third round, spread out all the cross sticks as evenly as possible.

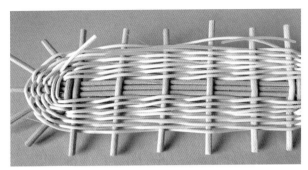

4. On round four, cut off one of the weavers and continue with the remaining rod, working over-one, under-one. At each new round, weave in front of two adjoining sticks first, as there is an even number of stakes. This will leave a small ridge (highlighted in orange, above) which will move forward one space with each round.

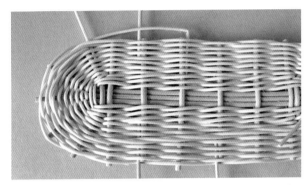

5. Finish the base by securing the weaver. Fold and tuck it into the weave.

6. Insert the stakes into the middle section of the base. Here, the four stakes run right across the width of the base.

On the rounded ends of the oval, the stakes are inserted either side of the base sticks (in the same way as on the round slath base).

Crossover base

This is a more supple base. Unlike the slath base, the length of the rods here is equivalent to the diameter of the base + twice the height of the sides + twice the length of the border.

3. Work four rounds in this way, with the weaver following the same path each round. Hold the weaver between two stakes.

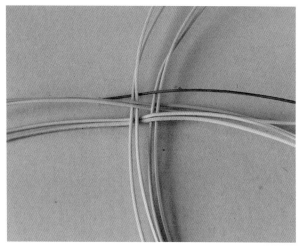

1. Cut eight rods to the appropriate length (see above). Mark the mid-point of each with a pencil. Arrange four sets of two rods, intersecting at the centre as shown. Insert the end of one weaver.

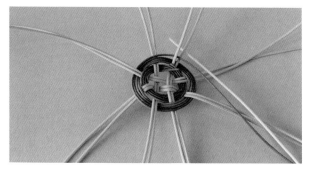

4. Add one new weaver to start a pairing weave (see page 18).

2. Weave in a circle, over-and-under, clockwise, for four rounds to create the centre. Then twist the weaver and weave in the opposite direction, anticlockwise, from right to left.

5. Separate each spoke, and continue the pairing weave to the required circumference of the base.

Josephine knot base

Like the crossover base, the Josephine knot base is supple and very decorative. The rods in the knot form the stakes to support the weave, and are later twisted together to create the border.

3. Once you have made the flat knot, tighten it up and keep the knot centred.

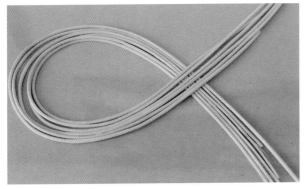

1. Cut two pairs of six rods, each 2.5mm (³/₃₂in) diameter, gather the first six rods into a bundle and form a simple loop.

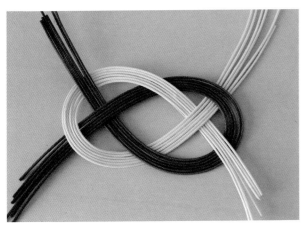

2. To form the knot, connect a second bundle of six rods as shown, with each bundle passing over-and-under alternately.

4. Divide the bundles into pairs, and use a pairing weave to start the base, using a long weaver folded at the centre.

WEAVING THE SIDES

The sides of a basket – the 'siding' – can be made from a variety of different weaving 'strokes' through the stakes. Weavers should be of a finer diameter than the stakes (see Working rules, page 8).

Randing weave

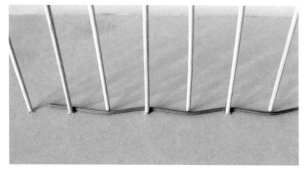

This is the simplest weave, and is used with an odd number of stakes. Place the weaver behind one stake, then weave in front, behind, and so on.

Two-rod slew

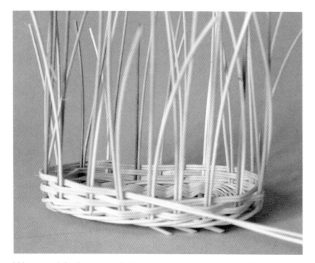

Weave this in exactly the same way as randing (above), but use two weavers together. In the USA, this is called 'double weaving'.

Pairing weave

This can be used with either an odd or even number of stakes, and gives you a nice rounded shape to the siding.

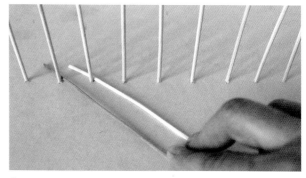

1. Use two weavers, one placed in each gap.

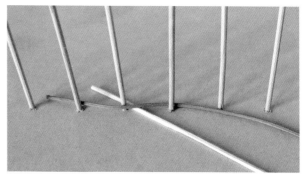

2. Start with the left-hand weaver (in pink, above); go in front of one stake and then continue in and out.

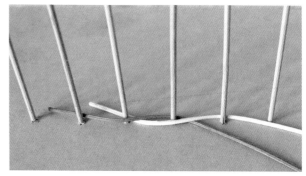

3. Work the second weaver (white) in the same way. The two weavers cross over in the gaps.

Triple weave

Also known as a three-rod wale, this stroke provides good rigidity. I use it at the base of some of my projects. It is denser than the pairing weave. In the US, this is also called 'triple twist'.

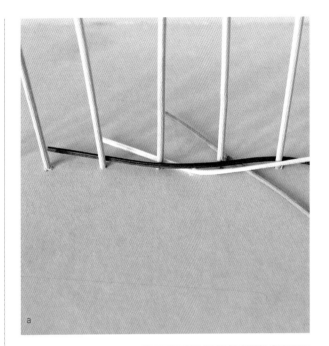
a

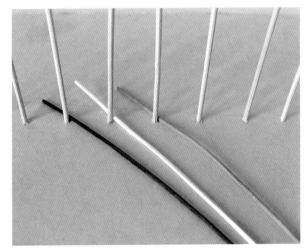

1. Use three weavers, and place one in each gap.

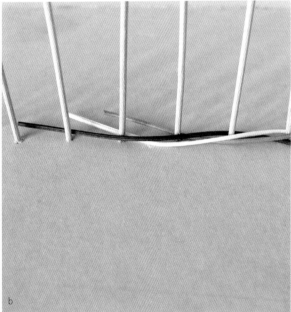
b

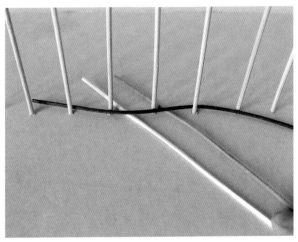

2. Start with the left-hand weaver (black); pass it in front of two stakes, then behind the next one, and back to the front.

3. Do the same with the white weaver (photograph a), and then the pink one (photograph b). Continue with the black.

SPLICING

When weaving, you will regularly need to connect (or 'splice') the end of one weaver and the start of another.

Fold over and insert the new weaver to the right of the previous stake, in the same gap.

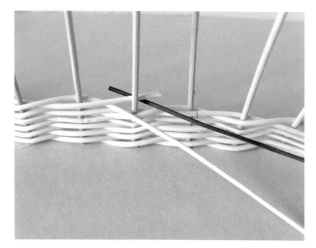

- **During a pairing weave:** the splice will be behind a stake, in the next gap. The new weaver is placed under the old one. Continue weaving first with the other weaver (the white one).

- **During a two-rod slewing weave:** always position the new weaver above the remaining one (that is, the one that is not yet finished) and behind the same stake.

- **During a triple weave:** fold and tuck in the weaver to the left of the next stake.

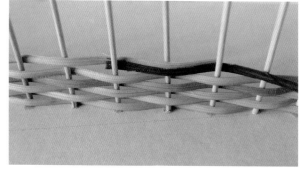

- **When weaving with lapping cane:** the new weaver runs alongside the old one for 5–7cm (2–2¾in).

BORDERS

The border provides a natural finish to the siding and gives the piece rigidity. Making a border involves weaving together the stakes, so it is essential to moisten them carefully before you start.

Scallop border

The scallop border is a simple weave created in two stages:

- **First stage:** fold down each stake behind the next one, towards the outside of the basket.

Place the last stake in the adjacent gap: i.e., underneath the first folded stake.

- **Second stage:** Re-insert each stake in front of the next two stakes so that it sits against the third stake. When you're done, all the stakes will be pointing inside the basket.

Three-rod plain border

This is a more elaborate interlaced border than the others. It takes a bit of practice, but will give your projects great rigidity. (We have numbered the stakes to make it clearer.)

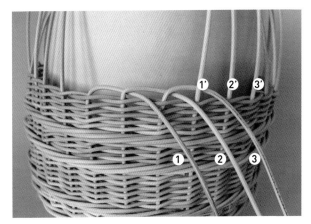

1. Successively bend down three stakes behind the respective adjacent stakes.

Important: Don't bend down these first stakes too tightly, as you will need to leave room for the final stakes to be inserted underneath them.

2. Bring stake 1 in front of the next two stakes, then behind the next one. Bend down stake 1' alongside stake 1.

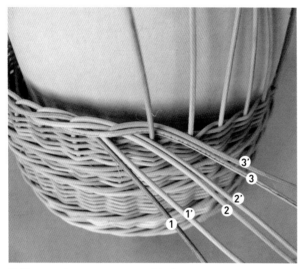

3. Repeat the same weave with the second and then the third stake: stake 2 and 2', and then stake 3 and 3'.

4. Continue the weave along the entire circumference, always taking the longest strand of the pair to the far left. Stake 6 has been placed in front of two stakes, and then underneath stake 1.

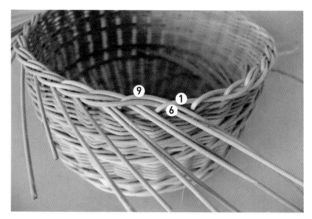

5. Bring down the final stake – 9 – next to stake 6.

6. The completed border: make sure you have three pairs. Place stake 7 in front of stake 1, behind the next stake, and then out again.

8. Place stake 9 in front of stake 3, behind the next stake, and then out again.

7. Place stake 8 in front of stake 2, behind the next stake and then out again.

9. From here, all the stakes are pointing outwards. Push them neatly back in one by one, underneath the border.

Trac border

This is a flexible border which interlaces stakes on the diagonal.

1. Bend down a pair of stakes and weave it in front of the next two pairs, then behind one pair, then in front of the next, then push it inside.

Important: don't push the first stakes down too tightly, as you will need to leave space for the final stakes to be inserted underneath them at the end.

2. Continue in the same way for each pair of stakes. The final pairs will be inserted in the space beneath the first pair of folded stakes.

3. Make sure all the stakes remain neat and parallel.

OTHER FEATURES

Hoops

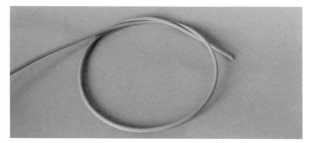

1. Twist together a long weaver to get a circle of the required diameter.

2. Twist one end of the weaver all around the ring.

3. Go around the ring a second time, to get a rope effect along the circumference.

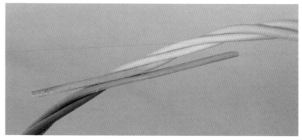

4. The two ends of the weaver should come together on the inside of the ring.

The 'God's Eye'

The God's Eye (or 'four-point lashing') is a beautiful knot feature. Use a long length of flat-oval lapping cane to avoid having to add further cane.

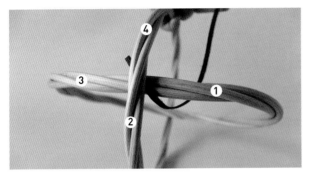

1. Trap the lapping cane between two hoops as above.

2. Wind the cane around side 1 from bottom to top. Place it diagonally onto side 2 and wind it around.

3. Continue like this on sides 3 and 4, working clockwise.

Underneath the start of the God's Eye.

4. For a good weave, keep an even tension.

5. Each round supports the next one, so be sure to place the cane right alongside each previous round.

FINISHING TECHNIQUES

When the basket is completely dry, after twelve to twenty-four hours depending on the size of your work, you need to cut off any protruding ends. Place your scissors, shears or secateurs flush with the weave, and cut each strand. The trimmed end must always rest against a stake to avoid the weave coming undone.

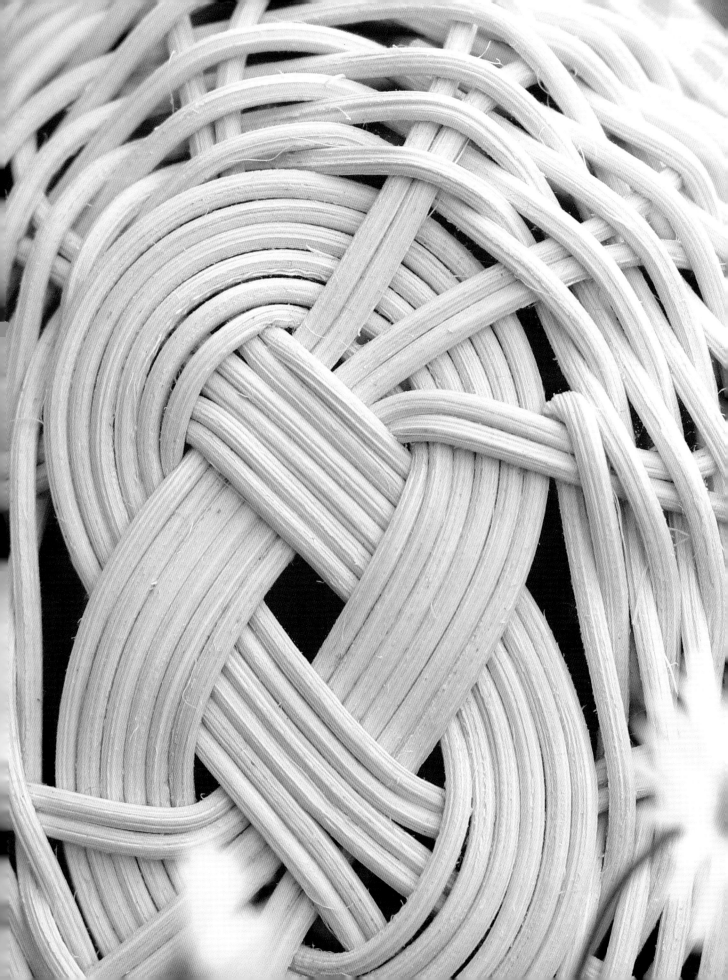

PROJECTS

CHAPTER 1
BAGS & BANGLES

COUNTRY BASKET

Have you ever had a go at frame basketry? Here's your chance, with this traditional country-style basket woven with plenty of colour to give it a light, fresh appeal.

MATERIALS

- Lengths of undyed cane of 2mm ($^1/_{16}$in), 2.5mm ($^3/_{32}$in) and 6mm ($^1/_4$in) diameter
- Flat-oval lapping cane in violet

Size of the completed basket: 22cm (8¾in) high by 30cm (11¾in) diameter.

INSTRUCTIONS

Hoops

1. Use long flexible rods, about 6mm (¼in) diameter, to make two different-sized rings. The first will be 30cm (11¾in) diameter, and the second is 22cm (8¾in) (see page 24).

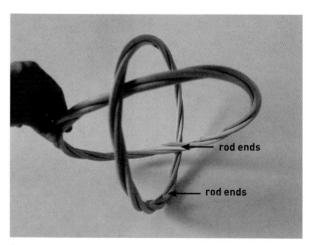

rod ends

rod ends

2. Insert the larger ring into the smaller one (as shown above) so that it becomes wedged in place. Check that the rod ends are located exactly as shown above.

Making the God's Eye

3. Secure a long violet lapping cane between the two rings and weave the 'eye' clockwise for three complete rounds (see page 25).

4. Insert into the eye a fine 2mm (¹⁄₁₆in) weaver rod to the right of the violet strip, and continue to wind the eye for a further three rounds with the weaver and the purple cane side-by-side.

5. Secure the 2mm (¹⁄₁₆in) rod by wedging it into the ring, and then continue for three further rounds using just the purple cane, then wedge it in securely but do not cut it.

6. Before starting the second eye, check that the two parts of the basket are lined up equally.

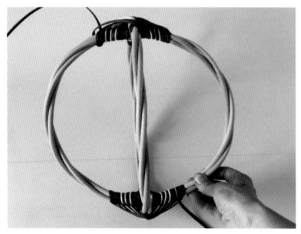

7. Create the second eye in exactly the same way as the first one.

Placing the ribs

8. Cut six ribs to size using the following lengths:

- two ribs of 41cm (16¼in) (1 and 6);
- two ribs of 39cm (15¼in) (2 and 5) and
- two ribs of 37cm (14½in) (3 and 4).

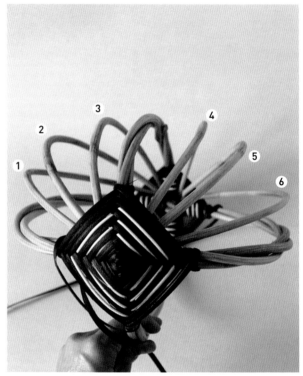

9. Place the ribs either side of one of the hoops, three to the right and three to the left. Place them securely against the two God's Eyes.

10. Arrange the ribs to get an even profile all the way around the basket.

Weaving the basket

To maintain a balanced shape, alternate your weaving between each side of the basket (see also page 44).

11. Soak the length of remaining lapping cane, and make a simple randing weave: under-one, over-one.

12. Weave back-and-forth three times with the violet cane, then a further three times doubling up the violet cane and a 2mm (¹⁄₁₆in) undyed cane rod, then a final three rows back and forth with the violet cane alone.

13. Cut the violet cane and continue weaving with a double rod of 2.5mm (³⁄₃₂in) undyed cane, placed over the violet cane and under two ribs to secure it.

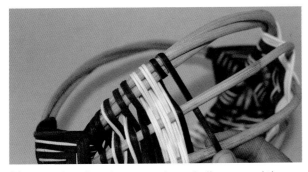

14. At each end, make a complete winding around the basket's rim, and then return.

15. Weave six back-and-forth rows with the 2.5mm (³⁄₃₂in) double strand.

16. Cut and then swap the double strand for the violet cane, and weave a further eight rows, back-and-forth.

17. Cut and then swap the violet strand for the 2.5mm (³⁄₃₂in) double strand and weave a further six rows, back-and-forth.

18. Weave back and forth across three ribs, and then two ribs (if required), to fill in any gaps – a technique called 'packing'.

Finishing

19. Leave to dry for twenty-four hours at room temperature, away from direct sunlight. Trim off any ends (see page 25).

HANDBAG

This handbag, with its red leather handles and diamond weave pattern, is full of vintage charm – and could become one of your wardrobe favourites.

MATERIALS

Base

- 4 base sticks, 28cm (11in) long, in 6mm (¼in) undyed cane
- 7 cross pieces, 19cm (7½in) long, in 6mm (¼in) undyed cane
- Lengths of 2mm (¹⁄₁₆in) and 2.5mm (³⁄₃₂in) undyed cane
- Lapping cane in red

Siding

- 32 side stakes, 48cm (19in) long, in 2.5mm (³⁄₃₂in) undyed cane – 8cm (3¼in) to insert + 20cm (7¾in) siding + 20cm (7¾in) for the border
- 3 side stakes, 99cm (39in) long, in 2.5mm (³⁄₃₂in) undyed cane: 19cm (7½in) + 2 x 20cm (7¾in) for the siding + 2 x 20cm (7¾in) for the border
- 35 liners, 19cm (7½in) long, in 2.5mm (³⁄₃₂in) undyed cane
- Lengths of undyed cane in 2mm (¹⁄₁₆in) and 2.5mm (³⁄₃₂in) diameters
- Red plastic strap, 1cm (⁵⁄₈in) wide and around 300cm (10ft) long (or alternatively use red lapping cane)

Accessories

- Two handles in red leather, 40cm (15¾in) long

Size of the finished handbag: 21cm (8¼in) high by 38cm (15in) wide (when fully open).

INSTRUCTIONS

Base

1. Make an oval slath base (see page 15). Begin the weave with 2mm (¹⁄₁₆in) undyed cane, moving up to 2.5mm (³⁄₃₂in) to finish.

2. Insert the thirty-two side stakes into the base, and the three long stakes which run all the way through the bottom of the base (see photograph on page 15).

3. Weave the upsett (see page 14) using four 100cm (39¼in) lengths of 2.5mm (³⁄₃₂in) undyed cane, and then prick up the side stakes.

Siding

4. Weave six rounds with triple weave (see page 19) using 2.5mm (³/₃₂in) undyed cane. Try to control the emerging silhouette of the bag by grouping together the opposite sets of stakes.

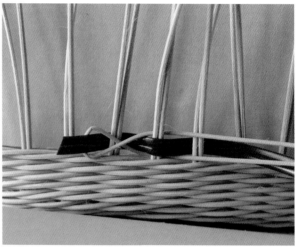

6. Cross over the two rods of cane, and bring them behind the next stake. Weave the plastic strip in front, and then behind the stakes. Continue in this way along the rest of the stakes.

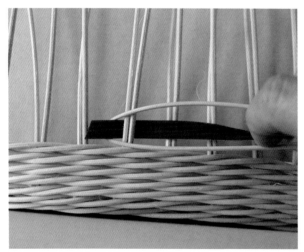

5. Double up each stake by adding the liners. Now make three rows of diamond weave: to do this, fold in half a long strand of 2mm (¹/₁₆in) cane. Place the red plastic strip behind one of the stakes, and block the loop of cane behind the red strip.

7. Make three further rounds of triple weave with 2.5mm (³/₃₂in) undyed cane. Then start with a pairing weave (see page 18). Keep an eye on how the shape is developing during the next twenty-three rounds.

Border

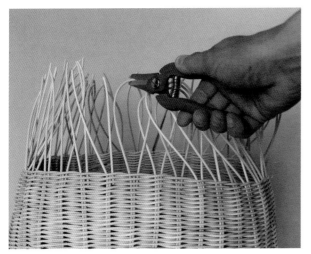

8. Take the end of each long stake and insert it securely back into the top of the side weave (as shown above) to form a loop. Then cut the top of each loop.

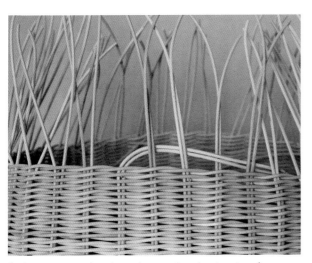

9. Create a trac border using each pair of stakes (see page 24).

Finishing

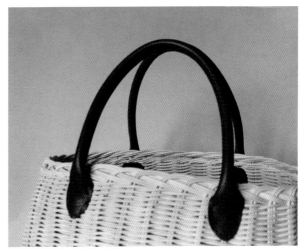

10. Let the work dry for twenty-four hours. Trim off any stubs (see page 25). Brush on some cane basketry varnish to both outside and inside. Centre, and then sew on, the two handles, using a robust thread as recommended by the supplier.

One handle, sewn on with robust thread.

BRACELETS

Cane accessories are a thing! Whether it's an everyday bangle or something special to wear on a night out, a cane bracelet will get you noticed. Use vibrant dyed colours or the simple unadorned beauty of undyed cane – the choice is yours.

> **Top tip**
> You can add extra zest to your piece by colouring the back of a cane strip using an indelible felt-tip pen.

INSTRUCTIONS

Basic structure

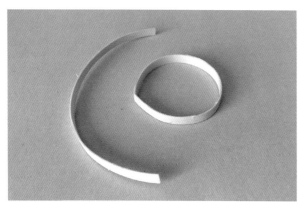

1. Measure around the widest part of your hand to make sure you will be able to put the bracelet on – on my hand, this measurement is 27cm (10¾in). Cut the first band. Place end-to-end and apply sticky tape to form the first bracelet.

2. Place a second band around the first and stick them together with a piece of tape.

FIRST BRACELET

MATERIALS

- 2 strips of flat band cane, 1cm (⅝in) wide and 30cm (11¾in) long (cut to length to suit your hand size)
- 30cm (11¾in) of glossy lapping cane, 3mm (⅛in) wide
- 250cm (98½in) of glossy lapping cane, 3mm (⅛in) wide
- 100cm (39¼in) of undyed lapping cane and 100cm (39¼in) of green lapping cane for the decoration
- Sticky tape
- 1 bodkin or bradawl

Lapping the bracelet

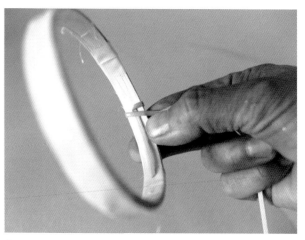

3. Fold the end of the glossy cane at a right angle and place it inside the bracelet. Then wind it around the bracelet three times.

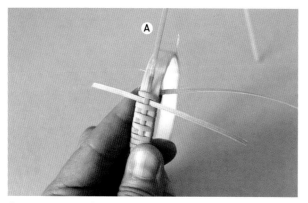

4. Slide a 30cm (11¾in) piece of cane (A) under the first three turns, and then resume lapping, alternately passing over and under cane A.

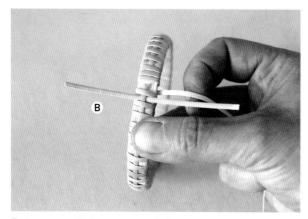

5. Carry on all the way round. On each turn, slide in a piece of cane (B) to allow space for the decorative strip later on.

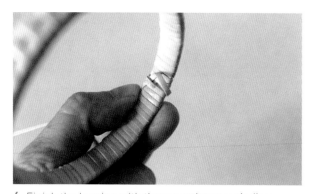

6. Finish the lapping with three continuous windings. Fold and insert the end of the lapping cane back where you started.

Decorating the bracelet

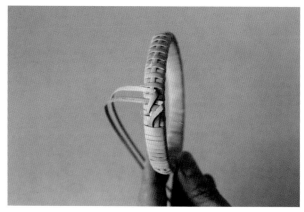

7. Secure the end of the first lapping cane under the continuously wrapped section. Work the undyed cane through every other gap.

8. Secure the end of the green cane in the same way as above, and work it through every other gap.

9. Continue round the entire circumference of the bracelet, alternating the undyed and green cane.

10. Finish off by using a bodkin to insert the end of the undyed cane into the continuously wound section, and then trim it off neatly.

Finishing

11. Leave it to dry for twelve hours. To add a little shine, polish the bracelet with a soft cloth.

SECOND BRACELET

MATERIALS

- 2 strips of flat band cane, 1cm (⅝in) wide and 30cm (11¾in) long (cut to fit your hand size)
- 30cm (11¾in) of glossy lapping cane, 3mm (⅛in) wide
- 250cm (98½in) of glossy lapping cane, very wide
- 150cm (59in) of undyed lapping cane for the decoration
- Sticky tape
- 1 bodkin

INSTRUCTIONS

Basic structure and lapping

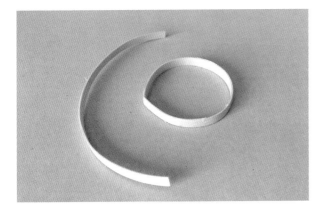

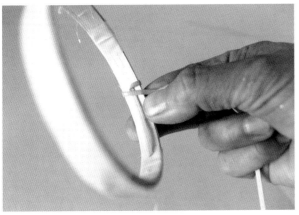

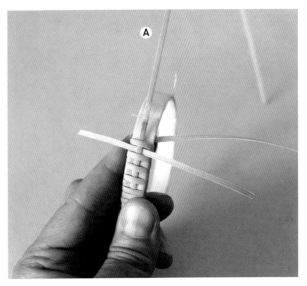

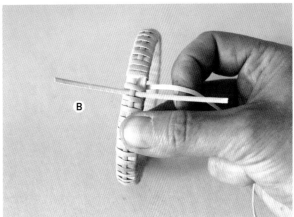

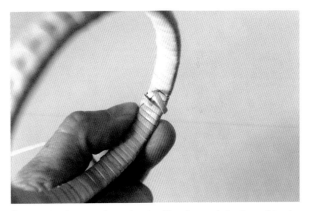

1. See the instructions for the first bracelet, steps 1 to 6.

Decoration

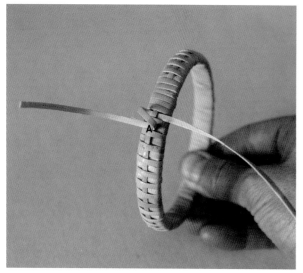

2. Leave 5cm (2in) of cane free (on the left side), and slide the other end under the central strip (A), loop it round to the left, and slide in the next gap above point A, from left to right.

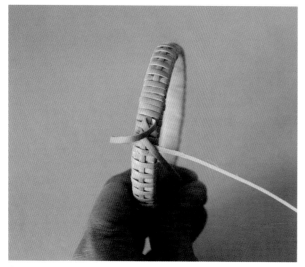

3. Fold down the free short end and hold it in place (to trim off later). Slide the cane under the central strip again from left to right, this time in the gap below point A. Now slide the cane under the central strip from left to right, this time at position A. In this way, the cane will pass twice through each gap.

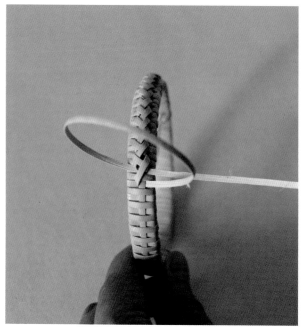

4. Continue in this way: down two gaps and through left-to-right; back up one gap and through left-to-right; down two gaps, etc.) around the whole bracelet.

5. Push the end of the decorative lapping cane underneath the central strip (A) using a bodkin, and cut off neatly.

Finishing

6. Leave to dry for twelve hours. As with the first bracelet, use a soft cloth to bring out a slight shine.

KNITTING BASKET

The fascinating handle in the form of a knot is an outstanding feature of this basket, but you'll need a bit of practice at making rib baskets to achieve an even weave and good shaping. The hot colours add a nice on-trend touch.

MATERIALS

- 2 x 5 rods, 140cm (55in) long of 4mm (¹¹⁄₆₄in) undyed cane
- Lengths of 2mm (¹⁄₁₆in) cane in undyed and mustard
- Lengths of lapping cane in undyed, yellow and brown

Size of completed basket: 27cm (10¾in) diameter.

INSTRUCTIONS

The Josephine knot

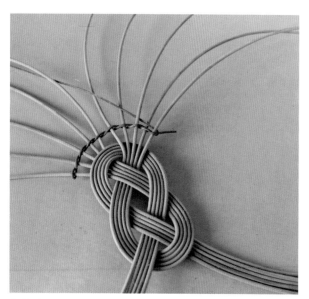

1. Make the base using a Josephine knot with two sets of five rods of undyed cane (see page 17). Separate the clusters of ten rods and keep them evenly spaced with one back-and-forth row of pairing weave (see page 18).

Siding

To get the best result, it is preferable to alternate your work between the two opposite sides, as you did with the country basket (see page 33). You won't be able to work them both at the same time.

2. Weave back and forth randing, to create 2cm (¾in) of siding, using a single mustard-coloured cane. Twist the weaver at each return to avoid it breaking.

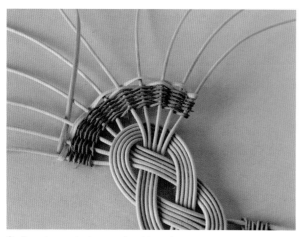

3. Cut the end of an undyed lapping cane to a point, so you can start the weave without adding bulk, and continue randing.

4. Carry on, adding 4cm (1½in) to each side.

Creating the shape

5. Cut the twenty rod ends to a point, and then insert them firmly into the weave directly opposite to create twin pairs of ribs, giving the basket its shape. The opening of the basket should be around 17cm (6¾in). Adjust the length of the ribs to create a pleasing ball shape, with the six central ribs at the same level to provide a flat base.

6. Continue weaving over the doubled ribs for a further 1cm (⅝in) using the brown lapping cane, and then 3cm (1¼in) with the yellow lapping cane.

7. Weave a further 1cm (⅝in) with the undyed 2mm (1/16in) cane, this time separating the doubled ribs.

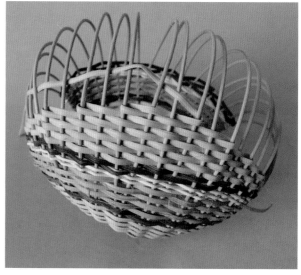

8. Build up the weave towards the centre using extra short rows ('packing') with the undyed lapping cane, aiming to keep both sides of the basket parallel as they come together.

9. Complete the weave, adding further short packing rows where needed, until the two sides meet neatly with no gaps.

Finishing

10. Leave the basket to dry for twenty-four hours at room temperature, away from direct sunlight. Trim off any stubs flush with the work (see page 25).

CHAPTER II
FOR THE KITCHEN

BREAD BASKET

This lovely heart-shaped bread basket can accompany your every meal. The cane webbing on the base adds a nice 'basketry' touch.

MATERIALS

- 1 heart-shaped base in plywood, 25cm (9¾in) wide
- 1 50 x 50cm (19¾ x 19¾in) piece of cane webbing
- Wood glue
- Red acrylic paint
- 41 rods, 45cm (17¾in) long of 2mm (¹/₁₆in) undyed cane – 20cm (7¾in) for the base border + 5cm (2in) siding + 20cm (7¾in) for the top border
- Lengths of 2mm (¹/₁₆in) undyed cane
- Lapping cane in red
- Strong scissors or secateurs

Size of the finished bread basket: 7cm (2¾in) high.

INSTRUCTIONS

Base

1. Paint the two sides of the heart red. Make sure not to block the holes in the plywood.

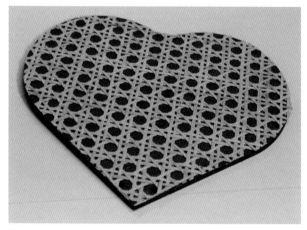

2. Apply a generous coating of wood glue to one side of the base. Glue on the cane webbing, and keep it pressed down for twelve hours. Carefully cut off any surplus webbing with strong scissors.

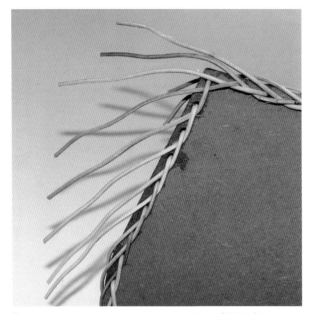

3. Insert the forty-one rods – each 45cm (17¾in) long – into their respective holes, and allow 20cm (7¾in) to extend beneath to make the base border. Fold down each rod under the next one to block it in place.

4. To cover the width of the plywood, weave as follows: in front of three, behind one, in front of one, then secure the end behind the next stake.

Weaving

5. Start the weave using a two-rod slew (see page 18), but using one lapping cane (cutting its end diagonally) and one rod of 2mm (¹⁄₁₆in) undyed cane. For best results, start the weave in the 'dip' part of the heart shape.

6. Weave seven rounds of randing, making sure the weave stays nice and straight.

Border

7. Soak the exposed stakes in water (not the siding), and make a three-rod plain border (see page 21).

Finishing

8. Leave to dry for twenty-four hours. Trim off any stubs (see page 25). Apply one coat of acrylic varnish to both the inside and outside of the basket.

SERVING MAT AND NAPKIN RINGS

Our lovely collection of bright colours will be perfect for showing off your home baking.

SERVING MAT

MATERIALS

Base

- 10 cross sticks, 30cm (11¾in) long, in 6mm (¼in) undyed cane
- 1 length of 2mm (¹⁄₁₆in) undyed cane
- 3 rods, 40cm (15¾in) long, in 2mm (¹⁄₁₆in) undyed cane

Siding

- Lengths of 2mm (¹⁄₁₆in) cane in yellow, orange, red, green, blue, violet and brown
- Lengths of undyed cane in 2mm (¹⁄₁₆in) and 2.5mm (³⁄₃₂in) diameters
- 4 rods, 115cm (45¼in) long, in 2.5mm (³⁄₃₂in) undyed cane for the upsett

Border

- 40 rods, 30cm (11¾in) long, in 2.5mm (³⁄₃₂in) undyed cane – 20cm (7¾in) for the border + 10cm (4in) to insert

**Size of the finished serving mat:
32cm (12½in) diameter.**

INSTRUCTIONS

Base

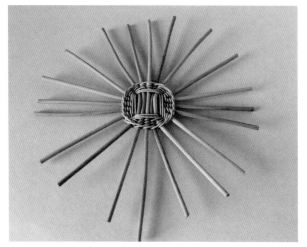

1. Start with a round slath base using the ten cross sticks (see page 12). Secure the spokes with a waling weave (see page 14) using the four rods of 2.5mm (³/₃₂in) undyed cane.

2. Weave two rounds of pairing (see page 18) with the yellow cane and cut the ends. Then weave two rounds pairing with 2mm (¹/₁₆in) undyed cane, then alternate two rounds of colour with two rounds of undyed cane each time.

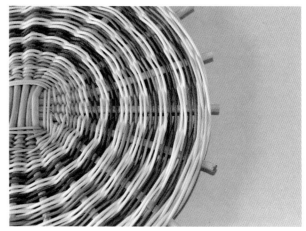

3. When the weaving is complete with all seven colours, finish with two rounds of triple weave (see page 19) with three rods of 2.5mm (³/₃₂in) undyed cane.

Border

4. Trim off the spokes flush with the weave. Then insert the forty rods of 2.5mm (³/₃₂in) cane 10cm (4in) into the edge of the weave, and make a three-rod plain border (see page 21).

Finishing

5. Leave to dry for twenty-four hours. Trim off any stub ends (see page 25). Brush on a coat of acrylic varnish to both sides of the mat.

NAPKIN RINGS

MATERIALS FOR ONE NAPKIN RING

- 8 rods, 20cm (7¾in) long, of 2.5mm (³⁄₃₂in) undyed cane
- Lengths of 2mm (¹⁄₁₆in) cane in yellow, orange, red, green, blue and violet
- A piece of PVC pipe, 4cm (1½in) diameter

Size of the finished napkin ring: 7cm (2¾in) high.

INSTRUCTIONS

1. Use an elastic band to hold all eight stakes around the pipe. Take a coloured weaver and fold it in half. Start a pairing weave (see page 18). After the first round, adjust the stakes so that they extend 7cm (2¾in) below the weave.

2. Make six rounds of pairing in total, and lock the final strand into the weave. You can now remove the pipe.

Border

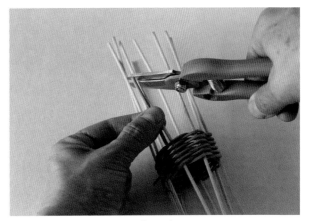

3. Trim the stakes to 7cm (2¾in) above and below the weave, using a 7cm (2¾in) piece of weaving cane as a measure.

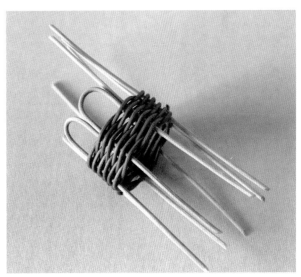

4. Soak the napkin ring in warm water. Fold over each stake in turn, inserting it into the weave alongside the next stake.

Finishing

5. Leave to dry for twenty-four hours. Brush on a single coat of acrylic varnish to the outside of the ring.

6. Go back to step 1 and make a new ring in a different colour. Make six rings to complete the set.

UTENSIL POT

With its angled sides and wide, stable base, this charming pot will keep all your cooking utensils exactly where you need them.

MATERIALS

Base

- 3 long sticks, 17cm (6¾in) long, in 4mm (¹¹⁄₆₄in) undyed cane
- 7 cross sticks, 9cm (3½in) long, in 4mm (¹¹⁄₆₄in) undyed cane
- 4 rods, 62cm (24½in) long, in 2.5mm (³⁄₃₂in) undyed cane, for the upsett
- 14 stakes, 35cm (13¾in) long, in 2.5mm (³⁄₃₂in) undyed cane – 3cm (1¼in) to insert + 12cm (4¾in) siding + 20cm (7¾in) for the border
- 3 stakes, 73cm (28¾in) long, in 2.5mm (³⁄₃₂in) undyed cane – 9cm (3½in) to insert + 2 x 12cm (4¾in) siding + 2 x 20cm (7¾in) border)

Siding

- 20 liners, 12cm (4¾in) long, in 2.5mm (³⁄₃₂in) undyed cane
- Lengths of 2mm (¹⁄₁₆in) undyed cane

Decorative border

- 3 rods, 57cm (22½in) long, in 2.5mm (³⁄₃₂in) undyed cane
- 1 rod, 42cm (16½in) long, in 3mm (⅛in) brown cane
- 1 hoop, 5cm (2in) diameter, in 3mm (⅛in) brown cane

Size of the finished pot: 14cm (5½in) diameter at the top by 13cm (5in) high.

INSTRUCTIONS

Base

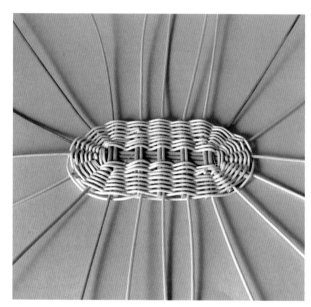

1. Start with an oval slath base (see page 15) using the long sticks and the cross sticks. Insert the fourteen stakes into the base, with seven at each end, one for each base stick in the rounded sections. Then insert the three long stakes that run right through the base alongside the three central cross sticks.

2. Weave the upsett (see page 14) with the four rods of 62cm (24½in) cane. Prick up the stakes to the vertical position.

Siding

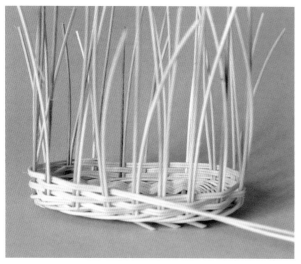

3. Double up the stakes by adding the twenty liners. Start the sides with a two-rod slew (see page 18) on one of the short sides, using two rods of 2mm (1/16in) undyed cane.

4. Slewing with an even number of stakes means you will need to jump across two stakes at the end of each round. Complete nineteen rounds in total.

5. Using the three rods of 57cm (22½in), weave the decorative border. The 42cm (16½in) strand of brown cane is simply entwined by the band of triple weave (see page 19), using the three rods of 2.5mm (3/32in) undyed cane.

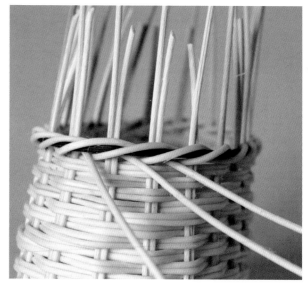

To hold the brown cane tightly, block off the rods of triple weave as you would for the upsett (see page 14).

6. Bring in two new rods of undyed cane on one of the short sides and make a further five rounds of two-rod slew. Trim off the liners close to the weave.

Border

7. Make a three-rod plain border (see page 21).

Adding the ring

8. Make a hoop (see page 24) that is 5cm (2in) diameter using 3mm (⅛in) brown cane. Fix the ring to the decorative band using a strand of 2mm (¹⁄₁₆in) undyed cane.

Finishing

9. Leave to dry for twenty-four hours. To allow for cleaning, brush on a coat of food-safe acrylic varnish to both inside and outside.

FRUIT BOWL

Basketweaving can be used to create things that are decorative as well as useful, and this lovely fruit bowl is no exception – ready to take pride of place in your kitchen.

MATERIALS

Base

- 8 base sticks, 25cm (9¾in) long, in 6mm (¼in) undyed cane
- 3 sticks, 9cm (3½in) long, in 6mm (¼in) undyed cane
- Lengths of 2mm (¹⁄₁₆in) cane in mustard yellow and lengths of 2.5mm (³⁄₃₂in) cane in raspberry pink for weaving the base
- 4 rods, 100cm (39¼in) long, of 2.5mm (³⁄₃₂in) raspberry pink cane for the upsett
- Short plugs of 6mm (¼in) cane
- 40 stakes, 35cm (13¾) long, in 2.5mm (³⁄₃₂in) raspberry pink cane

Siding

- 80 liners, 6cm (2¼in) long, in 2.5mm (³⁄₃₂in) undyed cane
- Lengths of 2mm (¹⁄₁₆in) cane in mustard yellow
- Lengths of 2.5mm (³⁄₃₂in) cane in raspberry pink
- 1 strip of flat band cane, 1.5cm (⅝in) wide by 95cm (37½in) long

Size of the finished basket: 25cm (9¾in) diameter by 8cm (3¼in) high.

INSTRUCTIONS

Base

Use a pairing weave for the base.

1. Make a round slath base (see page 12) with the eight cross sticks. Place the short plugs of 6mm (¼in) cane into the central gaps for even spacing.

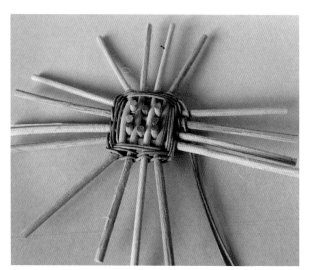

2. Use a pairing weave (see page 18) for three rounds with two rods of mustard colour cane.

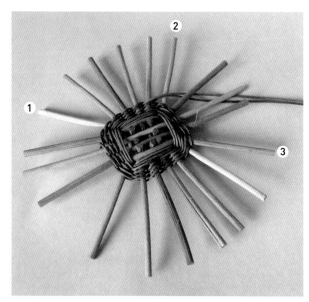

3. Insert the 9cm (3½in) sticks into three of the corners (1, 2 and 3 on the photograph).

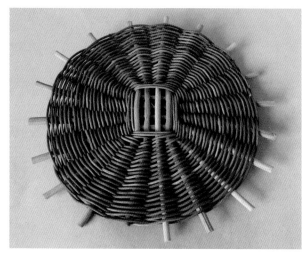

4. Work eight rounds in pairing weave with one rod of mustard and one rod of 2.5mm (³⁄₃₂in) raspberry. Finish the base weave with eight further rounds of pairing, this time using two rods of 2.5mm (³⁄₃₂in) raspberry pink cane.

5. Insert the forty side stakes and weave the upsett (see pages 13–14) using four rods, each 100cm (39¼in) long, in 2.5mm (³⁄₃₂in) raspberry pink cane. Prick up the side stakes.

Siding

6. Weave five rounds of triple weave (see page 19) with three rods of 2.5mm (³/₃₂in) cane in raspberry.

7. Insert the liners either side of each stake.

8. Weave one round of slewing (see page 18) using two rods of 2mm (¹/₁₆in) cane in mustard colour.

9. Weave one round using the flat band cane.

10. Weave another round of slewing with two rods of 2mm (¹/₁₆in) cane in mustard.

11. Finish weaving the basket with three rounds of triple weave using the raspberry pink cane.

Border

12. Make a three-rod plain border (see page 21).

Finishing

13. Leave to dry for twenty-four hours. To allow for cleaning, brush on a coat of food-safe acrylic varnish to both inside and outside.

PEDESTAL BOWL

This simple, contemporary bowl, made in
two parts, puts your most colourful fruits
and vegetables on a pedestal.

MATERIALS

Base

- 8 base sticks, 22cm (8¾in) long, in 6mm (¼in)
  undyed cane
- Lengths of 2mm (¹⁄₁₆in) and 2.5mm (³⁄₃₂in) undyed
  cane for the base weave
- 4 rods, 93cm (36½in) long, in 2.5mm (³⁄₃₂in)
  undyed cane for the upsett
- 32 stakes, 28cm (11in) long in 2.5mm (³⁄₃₂in) cane
  in raspberry pink – 7cm (2¾in) to insert + 3cm
  (1¼in) siding + 18cm (7in) of border

Siding

- 32 liners 21cm (8¼in) long, in 2.5mm (³⁄₃₂in)
  undyed cane
- 4 rods, 93cm (36½in) long, in 2.5mm (³⁄₃₂in)
  undyed cane for the decorative band
- Lengths of 2.5mm (³⁄₃₂in) undyed cane for
  the weave

The pedestal

- 16 stakes, 27cm (10¾in) long, in 2.5mm (³⁄₃₂in)
  undyed cane – 3cm (1¼in) to insert + 9cm (3½in)
  for the sides + 15cm (6in) for the border)
- Lengths of 2.5mm (³⁄₃₂in) undyed cane for weaving
  the pedestal
- 1 bodkin

**Size of the finished pedestal bowl: 26cm (10¼in)
diameter by 12cm (4¾in) high.**

INSTRUCTIONS

Base

1. Make a round slath base using the eight base sticks (see page 12).

2. Start with fifteen rounds of pairing weave using 2mm (¹⁄₁₆in) undyed cane, then six rounds pairing with 2.5mm (³⁄₃₂in) cane. Insert the thirty-two stakes and weave the upsett (see page 14) with the four rods 93cm (36½in) long. Prick up the side stakes.

Siding

3. Make three rounds of triple weave with the 2.5mm (³⁄₃₂in) undyed cane, and then the decorative band using four rods of 93cm (36½in). Double the stakes by adding the thirty-two liners.

Border

4. Make a trac border with the following sequence: in front of two pairs, behind one pair, in front of one pair. Bring the height of the first pair of stakes down to 1.5cm (⁵⁄₈in).

5. Interlace the final stakes into the 1.5cm (⁵⁄₈in) gap at the start of the border.

Pedestal

6. Soak the base of the basket. Using a bodkin, insert the sixteen pedestal stakes in a circle, 3.5cm (1½in) from the basket's centre.

7. Start with a pairing weave (see page 18). Flare out the stakes and control the shape carefully as you make the next sixteen rounds.

8. Weave three rounds of triple weave (see page 19), using 2.5mm (³⁄₃₂in) undyed cane. Complete the weave with a scallop border (see page 21).

Finishing

9. Leave to dry for twenty-four hours. To allow for cleaning, brush on a coat of food-safe acrylic varnish to both inside and outside.

CHAPTER III
FOR CHILDREN

STAR

This beautiful star can decorate your home as well as your Christmas tree. This project is also a great way to use up any spare offcuts in your cane stash!

MATERIALS

- 16 rods, 22cm (8¾in) long, in 2.5mm (³/₃₂in) undyed cane
- 16 rods, 22cm (8¾in) long, in 2.5mm (³/₃₂in) cane in red
- 12 small elastic bands, 6 in red, 6 in yellow

Size of the finished star: 22cm (8¾in).

INSTRUCTIONS

1. Make up six bunches of four rods each (two undyed and two red). Place the first three bunches in a triangle, as shown in the photograph above.

2. Place a fourth bunch of rods parallel to one of the first three so that it forms a second triangle.

3. Now position a fifth bunch to make a third triangle alongside the first two, as shown above.

5. Tighten up the centre by pushing in the bunches of cane and even out the shape.

4. Next, place a final bunch to make two further triangles. The centre of the arrangement now makes a hexagon. Make sure all the bunches are held firmly in place where they intersect.

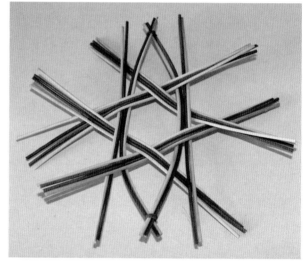

6. Take two rods from each of two parallel bunches, and join them at both ends with red elastic bands.

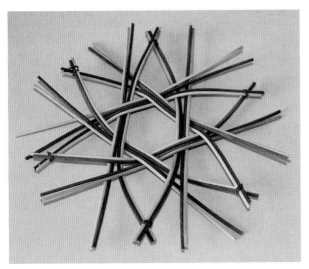

7. Do the same with the two other pairs of parallel bunches, using red elastic bands.

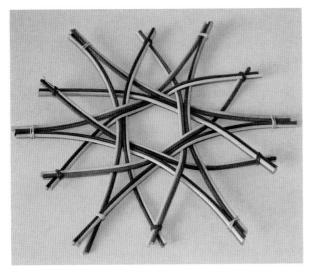

8. Now do the same with the three remaining pairs of parallel bunches of cane, this time using yellow elastic bands.

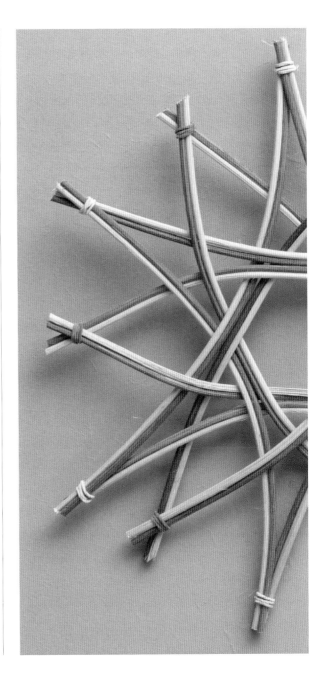

PENCIL POT

When the kids come home from school it's time to get creative – thanks to this lovely pot of pencils! This is a quick and colourful project – ideal for using up odd lengths of coloured cane.

MATERIALS

Base

- 16 rods, 60cm (23½in) long, in 2.5mm (³⁄₃₂in) undyed cane
- Lengths of 2mm (¹⁄₁₆in) cane for the base weave

Siding

- 48 liners, 10cm (4in) long in 2mm (¹⁄₁₆in) undyed cane (to make the 'spines')
- Offcuts of 2mm (¹⁄₁₆in) cane, minimum 20cm (7¾in) long, in a variety of colours

Size of the pencil pot: 10cm (4in) high and 9cm (3½in) wide.

INSTRUCTIONS

Base

1. Make a crossover base (see page 16) with eight of the 60cm (23½in) rods.

2. Then, make four rounds of pairing weave with one long rod in 2mm (¹⁄₁₆in) cane.

Siding

3. Prick up the stakes (the eight rods used for the base) and start with a triple weave (see page 19).

4. Using a variety of coloured offcuts, continue with fourteen rounds of triple weave.

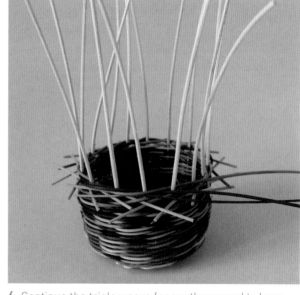

6. Continue the triple weave for another round to keep the spines in place.

5. Put aside the three weavers for the triple weave (don't cut them) and insert one 10cm (4in) liner horizontally behind each of the stakes, so that you have used sixteen in total.

7. Add another sixteen spines, then another row of triple, then sixteen more spines, and finish with five rows of triple weave.

Border

8. Push down each of the stakes in turn to create a scallop border (see page 21).

Finishing

9. Leave to dry for twenty-four hours. Trim off any protruding stubs (see page 25). Brush on a coat of acrylic varnish, both inside and outside.

EGG

This lovely egg with its Josephine knot base will delight the kids – especially if it's filled up with chocolates. You can decorate it with all kinds of coloured ribbons: just let your imagination run wild!

MATERIALS

- 2 x 12 rods, 50cm (19¾in) long, in 2mm (¹⁄₁₆in) undyed cane
- Lengths of 2mm (¹⁄₁₆in) undyed cane
- Decorative ribbons
- Elastic band

Size of the finished egg: 12cm (4¾in) high and 8cm (3¼in) wide.

INSTRUCTIONS

The Josephine knot base

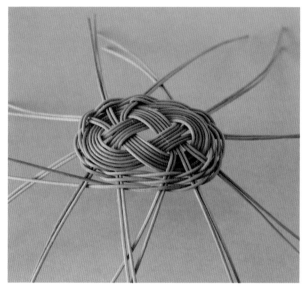

1. Make the Josephine knot base with two bunches of six rods of undyed cane (see page 17). Fold in half a single length of 2mm (¹⁄₁₆in) cane. Separate each bunch of six rods into three pairs, and start the pairing weave (see page 18). Make two rounds of pairing, keeping the weavers side-by-side for a flat finish.

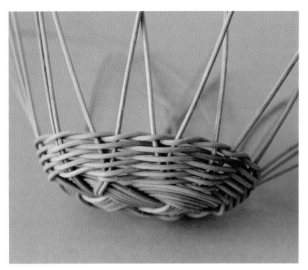

2. Bend up the stakes to give the rounded shape to the egg. Separate all the stakes and continue the pairing weave.

3. Weave two further rounds of pairing.

Border

4. Bring down each of the stakes in turn towards the outside to create a scallop border (see page 21).

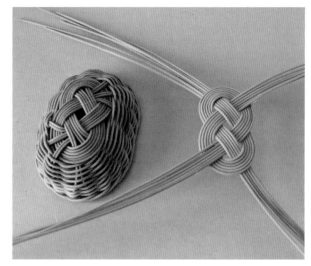

5. Make a second Josephine knot to make the second half of the egg, and follow steps 1–4 once again.

Finishing

6. Leave to dry for twelve hours. Trim off any stubs (see page 25). Brush on one coat of acrylic varnish to the inside and outside. Hold together the two halves of the egg with an elastic band and add ribbon embellishments.

BASKET ON WHEELS

This cute little basket on wheels will be a hit with any toddler who needs to get from A to B with teddies, rabbits and other furry friends. It's easy to make, too!

MATERIALS

Base

- 4 base sticks, 33cm (13in) long, in 6mm (¼in) undyed cane
- 7 cross sticks, 20cm (7¾in) long, in 6mm (¼in) undyed cane
- 4 rods, 116cm (45¾in) long, in 3mm (⅛in) undyed cane for the upsett
- Lengths of undyed cane in 2mm (¹⁄₁₆in), 2.5mm (³⁄₃₂in) and 3mm (⅛in) for the base weave
- 32 stakes, 56cm (22in) long, in 3mm (⅛in) undyed cane – 8cm (3¼in) to insert + 28cm (11in) sides + 20cm (7¾in) for the border
- 3 stakes, 116cm (45¾in) long, in 2.5mm (³⁄₃₂in) undyed cane – 20cm (7¾in) to insert + 2 x 28cm (11in) sides + 2 x 20cm (7¾in) for the border

Siding

- Lengths of 2.5mm (³⁄₃₂in) undyed cane
- Undyed lapping cane

Accessories

- 2 sets of 2 wooden wheels and axles
- Printed cotton fabric
- 50cm (19¾in) of string

Size of the finished basket: 35cm (13¾in) diameter (at the top) by 28cm (11in) high.

INSTRUCTIONS

Base

1. Make an oval slath base (see page 15) with the base sticks and cross sticks, using a pairing weave with 2mm (¹⁄₁₆in), 2.5mm (³⁄₃₂in) and 3mm (¹⁄₈in) cane. Insert the thirty-two 56cm (22in) long stakes, and the three 116cm (45¾in) long stakes, which pass right through the base from one side to the other.

2. Weave the upsett (see page 14) with four rods – 116cm (45¾in) long – of 3mm (¹⁄₈in) undyed cane, and then prick up the stakes.

Siding

3. Work seven rounds in triple weave (see page 19) with three rods of 2.5mm (³⁄₃₂in) undyed cane, starting on one of the short sides. Now taking the undyed lapping cane, start a randing weave (see page 18) opposite where you finished the triple weave. Place a second lapping cane in the previous gap (as shown above) and weave a further round of randing.

4. Resume with the first lapping cane and make a third round of randing, ensuring the weavers do not cross over each other.

5. Complete the basket with these two weaves, alternating the lapping cane and the 2.5mm (³⁄₃₂in) round cane, as follows:

- ten rounds of randing with lapping cane;
- three rounds of triple weave with round cane
- twenty-two rounds of randing with lapping cane;
- three rounds of triple weave with round cane;
- five rounds of randing with lapping cane; and
- three rounds of triple weave with round cane.

Border

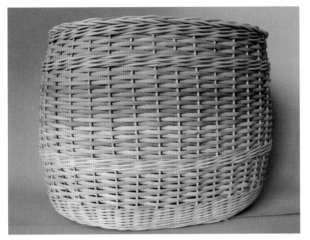

6. Create a three-rod plain border (see page 21).

Finishing

7. Leave to dry for twenty-four hours. Trim off any stubs (see page 25). Brush on one coat of acrylic varnish to the interior and exterior. Line the interior with fabric. Fix the two sets of wheels underneath the basket, and tie on a short cord to pull the basket along.

CHAPTER IV
FOR THE GARDEN

BIRD FEEDER

This cane bird feeder will look stunning in any garden. The birds will love it for a quick 'fly-thru' snack!

MATERIALS

- 8 base sticks, 80cm (31½in) long, in 2.5mm (³/₃₂in) undyed cane
- Lengths of 2mm (¹/₁₆in) undyed cane
- Lapping cane in khaki
- 4 liners, 12cm (4¾in) long, in 2.5mm (³/₃₂in) undyed cane to strengthen the 'doorways'
- 16 liners, 20cm (7¾in) long, in 2.5mm (³/₃₂in) undyed cane
- 2 hoops, 4.5cm (1¾in) diameter, in 2mm (¹/₁₆in) undyed cane
- 1 wire tie

Size of the finished feeder: 25cm (9¾in) high.

INSTRUCTIONS

Base

1. Make a crossover base (see page 16) with the eight base sticks.

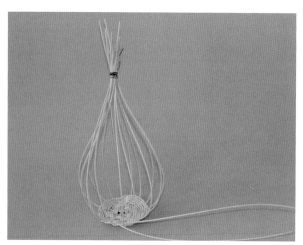

2. Weave a flat base with pairing (see page 18) for four rounds using 2mm (¹/₁₆in) undyed cane, then attach all eight stakes at the top to create the shape of the frame. Keep them in place with a wire tie.

Weave

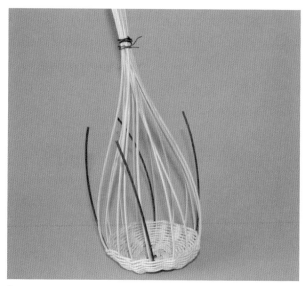

3. Continue pairing for a further six rounds, then insert the four liners, as shown above.

4. Use the khaki lapping cane in a randing weave (see page 18) to create the two side panels. Each one uses six stakes plus an additional liner on each side of the panel, so that a total of sixteen stakes are being used for both sides.

5. Make the two cane hoops (see page 24), leaving a free length of 30cm (11¾in) which you can use to 'stitch' the hoop to the side panel.

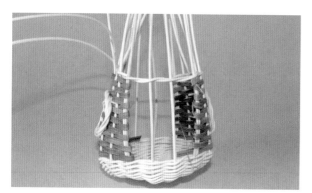

6. Start a new round of pairing weave using 2mm (¹⁄₁₆in) undyed cane, and continue on to make four rounds.

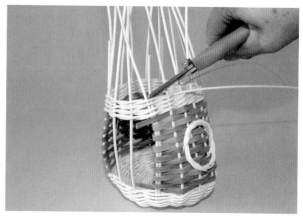

7. Trim the four liners flush with the weave.

8. Continue the pairing weave for a further fifteen rounds, gathering the stakes into pairs to help shape the weave to a conical point.

9. Cut off one of the two weavers and then tie up the stakes with three turns.

Doorways

10. Cut the stakes at the edge of the opening, one at the top, the other at the bottom. Bend each one and insert it into the weave. Do the same with the second opening.

Roof

11. Insert the sixteen liners alongside the stakes after the fourth row of pairing weave.

12. Start a new pairing weave above the existing weave, to create the eaves.

13. Continue with eight rounds, finish and block the ends into the weave. Bend each stake around, trim the end to a point and insert alongside the next liner.

14. Insert a long rod of 2mm (¹⁄₁₆in) undyed cane through the top of the feeder, making a ring to hang it up.

Finishing

15. Leave it to dry for twenty-four hours. Trim off any stubs (see page 25). Brush on some linseed oil to provide some weather protection.

CANDLE HOLDER

Nothing beats the light of a flickering candle when it comes to romantic evenings. Make this one, and you will also learn the elegant art of 'fitching' or openwork basketweaving.

MATERIALS

Base

- 8 sticks in 4mm (¹¹⁄₆₄in) undyed cane
- Lengths of 2mm (¹⁄₁₆in) and 2.5mm (³⁄₃₂in) undyed cane for the base weave
- 4 rods 65cm (25½in) long in 2.5mm (³⁄₃₂in) undyed cane for the upsett
- 32 stakes 35cm (13¾in) long in 2.5mm (³⁄₃₂in) undyed cane – 3cm (1¼in) to insert + 17cm (6¾in) sides + 15cm (6in) for the border

Siding

- 32 liners 15cm (6in) long in 2.5mm (³⁄₃₂in) undyed cane
- Lengths of 2mm (¹⁄₁₆in) and 2.5mm (³⁄₃₂in) undyed cane
- 1 glass candle holder 15cm (6in) diameter and 16cm (6¼in) high

Size of the finished piece: 17cm (6¾in) high.

INSTRUCTIONS

Base

1. Make a round slath base (see page 12) with the eight base sticks and then weave the base with 2mm (¹⁄₁₆in), and then 2.5mm (³⁄₃₂in), cane. Insert thirty-two stakes into the base weave.

2. Weave the upsett (see page 14) with the four 65cm (25½in) rods, and then prick up the stakes.

Siding

3. Start a triple weave with three rods of 2.5mm (³⁄₃₂in) undyed cane.

Insert one liner to the right of each stake to double the number of stakes. Insert the glass candle holder at this stage to keep your work to the right dimensions.

4. Fold a long 2mm (¹/₁₆in) undyed cane weaver in half, and start to secure the first round of fitching using a pairing weave. This needs some patience, as you need to get the stakes crossing regularly at the same height.

6. Fold in half a length of 2.5mm (³/₃₂in) undyed cane, add one further single 2.5mm (³/₃₂in) weaver, and begin a triple weave (see page 19) to secure the second level of fitching. The stakes are woven in pairs, but this time remain parallel, rather than crossing over.

5. Make a second round of pairing, and insert the ends into the siding to finish the round.

7. Weave two rounds of triple weave, leave the rods hanging, and cut the liners level with the weave, removing the candleholder to ensure an easier cut.

Border

8. Make a scallop border (see page 21) but with a slight variation because the stakes are very close together: first, fold down each stake behind the next two stakes.

9. Second, bring each stake in front of the next two stakes in the same way, and re-insert it.

Finishing

10. Leave to dry for twenty-four hours. Trim off all stubs flush with the work. You can use wood stain to add a deeper colour to the finished piece.

EGG BASKET

Making this charming and elegant egg basket will take time and patience, but is well worth it. This is a 'Zarzo' basket, an unusual design which originates in Spain. Take care to follow the instructions very closely.

MATERIALS

- 6 stakes, 100cm (39¼in) long, in 6mm (¼in) undyed cane
- Lengths of 2.5mm (³⁄₃₂in) undyed cane
- 2 x 6 rods, 80cm (31½in) long, in 3mm (⅛in) red cane
- 2 x 10 rods, 70cm (27½in) long, in 3mm (⅛in) undyed cane
- Undyed lapping cane for binding the handle
- 1 wire tie

Size of the egg basket: 25cm (9¾in) wide by 27cm (10¾in) high.

INSTRUCTIONS

Base

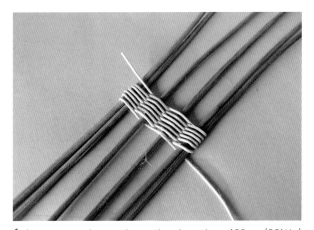

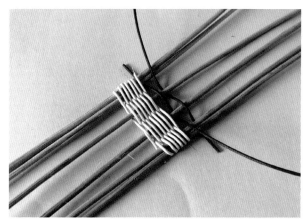

1. Lay out, as shown above, the six stakes, 100cm (39¼in) long in undyed cane, which will make the basket frame. In the centre, weave six rows randing back-and-forth with the length of 2.5mm (³⁄₃₂in) cane.

2. Weave the end of one red 3mm (⅛in) rod from left to right one row, and then take a second red rod and weave one row from right to left, as shown.

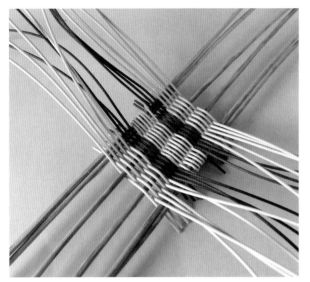

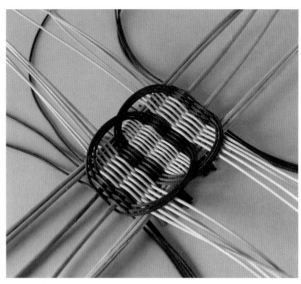

3. In the same way, weave the two sets of six red rods, and the two sets of ten undyed rods, either side of the central weave.

5. Continue to weave the two sets of six red rods, keeping the weave and bundles flat.

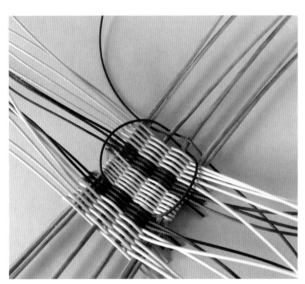

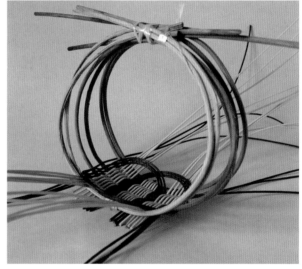

4. Pick up the first red rod and bring it over the central weave, making an arc, then continue the weave, remembering to alternate the rods (one row with a rod from the left, then one from the right, etc.).

6. Soak everything in water, then bring the softened stakes into a circle to form the basket frame. Hold everything together firmly with wire or tape at the top. Adjust the hoops to get a balanced frame shape.

Finishing the weave

7. Weave the two sets of ten undyed rods and the two sets of six red rods and then the two sets of ten undyed rods. Keep the rods evenly spaced.

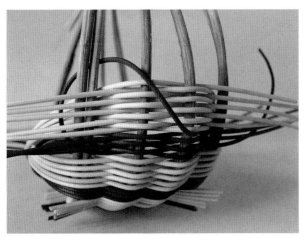

8. Bend the first red rod from the bottom, bring it behind the double stakes, and then insert it back through the weave opposite, passing in front of two stakes.

9. Continue to weave in all six red rods on each side, as shown. Trim off the undyed cane rods to follow the shape of the basket (see photograph).

Handle

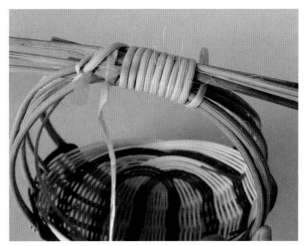

10. Fold over the end of the lapping cane and secure it between the rods. Bind the handle tightly for 7cm (2¾in), and push the free end into the binding using a bodkin.

Finishing

11. Leave to dry for twenty-four hours at room temperature, away from direct sunlight. Trim off any stubs (see page 25).

CHAPTER V
FOR THE HOME

PLANT POT HOLDER

The pot holder is a classic basketweaving project for the home, but this one has a modern twist, with the studded straps adding a nice contemporary touch.

MATERIALS

Base

- 8 base sticks, 16cm (6¼in) long, in undyed 6mm (¼in) cane
- 4 rods, 70cm (27½in) long, in 2.5mm (³⁄₃₂in) undyed cane for the upsett
- Lengths of 2mm (¹⁄₁₆in) and 2.5mm (³⁄₃₂in) undyed cane
- 32 stakes, 41cm (16¼in) long, in 3mm (⅛in) undyed cane – 5cm (2in) to insert + 16cm (6¼in) of siding + 20cm (7¾in) for the border

Siding

- 4 x 4 rods of 90cm (35½in) in 3mm (⅛in) undyed cane for the decorative bands
- Lengths of 2.5mm (³⁄₃₂in) undyed cane

Accessories

- 2 green straps, 1.5 x 90cm (⅝ x 35½in)
- 16 round-headed paper fasteners, around 7cm (2¾in) long and 12mm (½in) diameter

Size of the finished pot holder: 26cm (10¼in) diameter and 18cm (7in) high.

INSTRUCTIONS

Base

1. Make a round slath base (see page 12) with the eight base sticks, and work the base weave with 2mm (¹⁄₁₆in) and then 2.5mm (³⁄₃₂in) cane. Insert the thirty-two stakes in the base, either side of each of the base sticks.

2. Weave the upsett (see page 14) with the four 70cm (27½in) rods of undyed cane. Prick up the stakes.

Siding

3. Weave thirteen rounds of pairing (see page 18) using the two rods of 2.5mm (³⁄₃₂in) undyed cane.

4. Weave the decorative band as you would an upsett using four rods of 3mm (⅛in) undyed cane (see page 14). Then weave three rounds of pairing with the 2.5mm (³⁄₃₂in) undyed cane.

5. Weave a second decorative band, again using the four rods, 90cm (35½in) long, of undyed cane.

6. Weave six rounds pairing using two rods of 2.5mm (³⁄₃₂in) undyed cane.

7. Now weave two further decorative bands, separated this time by just three rounds of pairing.

Border

8. Create a three-rod plain border (see page 21).

Attaching the straps

9. Position the green straps between the two sets of decorative bands. Pierce them, and then push a paper fastener through both the weave and the strap to hold the strap in place. Insert eight paper fasteners into each strap.

Finishing

10. Leave to dry for twenty-four hours at room temperature, away from direct sunlight. Trim off any stubs (see page 25).

11. To protect the canework from humidity, apply a coat of acrylic varnish to the inside and outside. Placing a saucer at the bottom of the pot holder will help protect it from water.

WALL BASKET

Basketry can also be used to make attractive and original accessories for the home – like this beautiful wall basket with its openwork sides and decorative heart details.

MATERIALS

Base

- 3 base sticks, 18cm (7in) long, in 4mm ($^{11}/_{64}$in) undyed cane
- 7 cross sticks, 7cm (2¾in) long, in 4mm ($^{11}/_{64}$in) undyed cane
- 4 rods, 63cm (24¾in) long, in 2.5mm ($^{3}/_{32}$in) undyed cane for the upsett
- 28 stakes, 46cm (18in) long, in 2.5mm ($^{3}/_{32}$in) undyed cane – 4cm (1½in) to insert + 22cm (8¾in) siding + 20cm (7¾in) border
- 3 stakes, 93cm (36½in) long, in 2.5mm ($^{3}/_{32}$in) undyed cane – 9cm (3½in) to insert + 2 x 22cm (8¾in) siding + 2 x 20cm (7¾in) border

Siding

- 32 liners, 21cm (8¼in) long, in 2.5mm ($^{3}/_{32}$in) undyed cane
- 1 offcut from a strip of flat band cane 15mm ($^{5}/_{8}$in) wide
- Lengths of 2mm ($^{1}/_{16}$in) undyed cane for the weavers

Size of the finished wall basket: 25cm (9¾in) diameter at the top by 22cm (8¾in) high.

INSTRUCTIONS

Base

1. Start with an oval slath base (see page 15) using the base sticks and cross sticks, and make a base weave with 2mm (1/16in) cane. Insert the twenty-eight stakes – each 46cm (18in) – into the base, and the three longer stakes which will pass all the way through the base.

2. Make the upsett (see page 14) with the four 63cm (24¾in) rods, and then prick up the stakes to the vertical position.

Siding

3. Make six rounds of triple weave (see page 19) using three rods of 2mm (1/16in) undyed cane. Start on one of the short sides. Then double up each of the stakes by inserting the thirty-two liners.

Central weave

4. Using a single 2mm (1/16in) length of undyed cane, make eleven sets of back-and-forth rows of randing across the four central stakes.

5. Bring in a new length of undyed cane. Cross over each pair of stakes into an 'X' and hold them in place with a single row of pairing weave.

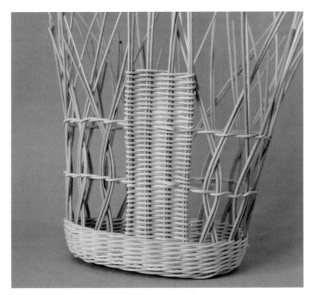

6. Repeat steps 4 and 5 to create a second and third level.

7. Weave five rounds of triple weave with three rods of 2mm (¹⁄₁₆in) undyed cane, starting on a short side.

Wall fixture

8. Insert a short piece of 1.5cm (⅝in) flat cane at the centre of the back of the basket, and make a final round of triple weave as shown.

Border

9. Make a three-rod plain border (see page 21).

Finishing

10. Leave to dry for twenty-four hours. Trim off any stubs (see page 25). Attach any decorative features, such as these ceramic hearts.

MIRROR

This beautiful vintage-style mirror with its double border should take pride of place in your home. It will take skill and patience to get it looking perfect, but is well worth it!

MATERIALS

Base

- 8 base sticks, 22cm (8¾in) long, in 6mm (¼in) undyed cane
- Lengths of 2mm (¹⁄₁₆in) and 2.5mm (³⁄₃₂in) undyed cane for the base weave

Border

- 32 liners, 40cm (15¾in) long, in 3mm (⅛in) undyed cane
- 32 liners, 40cm (15¾in) long, in 3mm (⅛in) brown cane
- 32 liners, 40cm (15¾in) long, in 3mm (⅛in) blue cane
- 32 liners, 25cm (9¾in) long, in 3mm (⅛in) blue cane for the border
- 3 rods, 85cm (33½in) long, in 2.5mm (³⁄₃₂in) undyed cane for the upsett
- Lengths of 2mm (¹⁄₁₆in) and 2.5mm (³⁄₃₂in) undyed cane

Accessories

- 1 mirror, 20cm (7¾in) diameter

Size of the finished mirror: 40cm (15¾in) diameter.

INSTRUCTIONS

Base

1. Make a round slath base with the eight base sticks (see page 12). Make fourteen rounds of pairing weave with the 2mm (¹⁄₁₆in) cane and five rounds with 2.5mm (³⁄₃₂in) cane. Check that the woven diameter fits the mirror size. Insert the thirty-two stakes into the base weave and prick them up, ready for the upsett.

2. Make one round of triple weave (see page 19) using three 85cm (33½in) rods.

Central border

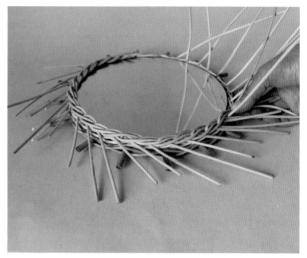

3. Place the mirror within the border. Soak the stakes (either with steam or a sponge) and make a three-rod plain border (see page 21).

4. To give the border a little more width, insert the ends back into the border.

Mirror border

5. Insert three liners (blue, brown, and undyed) either side of each of the sixteen base 'spokes' to make thirty-two three-rod bunches. Weave five rounds of pairing with 2.5mm (³/₃₂in) undyed cane.

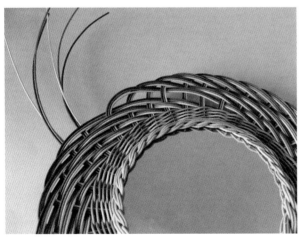

6. Bend over the bunch of three coloured rods 5.5cm (2¼in) from the pairing weave, and make a trac border as follows: in front of two, behind one, in front of two, behind one, in front of one, and finish behind.

Finishing

7. Leave to dry for twenty-four hours. Trim off any stubs (see page 25). Brush on one coat of acrylic varnish to both sides.

STORAGE BASKET

This roomy basket made with a mix of broad cane strips and cording is great to look at and extremely useful – weave it in whatever colours you like, and it will grace any room in the house.

MATERIALS

Base

- 4 base sticks, 32cm (12½in) long, in 6mm (¼in) undyed cane
- 7 cross sticks, 19cm (7½in) long, in 6mm (¼in) undyed cane
- Lengths of undyed cane in 2mm (¹⁄₁₆in), 2.5mm (³⁄₃₂in) and 3mm (⅛in) for the base weave
- 2 rods, 110cm (43¼in) long, in 2.5mm (³⁄₃₂in) undyed cane for the upsett
- 10 stakes, 45cm (17¾in) long, in undyed flat band cane 1.5cm (⅝in) wide for the front and back of the basket – 5cm (2in) to insert + 32cm (12½in) siding + 8cm (3¼in) border
- 14 stakes, 50cm (19¾in) long, in undyed flat band cane 1.5cm (⅝in) wide for the basket sides – 5cm (2in) to insert + 37cm (14½in) siding + 8cm (3¼in) border

Siding

- Lapping cane in undyed, khaki and brown
- Thick natural cord in green
- Flat band cane, 1cm (½in) wide, in khaki
- Flat band cane, 1.5cm (⅝in) wide, undyed
- Clothes pegs
- Lengths of undyed cane, 2mm (¹⁄₁₆in) diameter

Size of the finished basket: 33cm (13in) long by 38cm (15in) high.

INSTRUCTIONS

Base

1. Start with an oval slath base (see page 15) using the base sticks and cross sticks, and weave the base with the 2mm (¹⁄₁₆in), and then 3mm (⅛in) cane. Cut the ends of the twenty-four flat stakes to a sharp point, and using a bodkin insert them all into the base. Take care to insert the long stakes at the sides, and the shorter stakes to the front and back of the base oval.

2. This time, the upsett will be made with a pairing weave (see page 18) using two rods, 110cm (43¼in) long. Prick up all the stakes.

Siding

3. Weave six rounds of randing (see page 18) using two undyed lapping canes (see the Basket on Wheels, pages 84–87). Start on one of the short sides. Cut one long piece of green natural cord to a length equal to six times the circumference of the basket, plus 10cm (4in). Fold it equally in two, and on one of the short sides of the basket start a pairing weave (see page 18) for three rounds.

4. Use a randing weave (see page 18) for the different types of cane, and cut each one at the end of each round. Work as follows:

- three rounds in 1cm (½in) wide undyed cane strips;
- two rounds in khaki lapping;
- three rounds pairing weave using the green cord;
- three rounds in khaki lapping;
- three rounds in 1cm (½in) wide flat band cane, undyed;

- three rounds in 1cm (½in) wide flat band cane, khaki;
- one round in 1.5cm (⅝in) wide flat band cane, undyed; and
- three rounds in 1cm (½in) wide flat band cane, khaki.

Using the brown lapping cane, 'embroider' the criss-cross design either side of the 1.5cm (⅝in) wide undyed cane strip.
Weave three rounds in 1cm (½in) wide undyed cane strip.
Weave three rounds of pairing weave using the green cord.

5. Using the undyed lapping cane, alternating with the 1.5cm (⅝in) wide undyed cane strip, weave a 'packing' triangle on each side (see above) so that the rounded edges of the basket are higher than the sides.

Sewn border

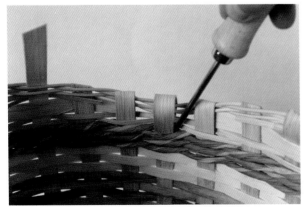

6. Before starting the border, make two rounds of pairing weave with the 2mm (¹⁄₁₆in) undyed cane. Bend over three out of every four flat stakes and insert them into the weave. Cut the remaining stakes flush with the weave.

7. Position two strips of cane 1cm (½in) wide around the inside of the rim, and two khaki strips 1cm (½in) wide around the outside, holding them all in place with clothes pegs as shown above. Using undyed lapping cane, sew around all the bands to secure them.

Finishing

8. Leave to dry for twenty-four hours. Cut off any stub ends (see page 25). Brush on a coat of acrylic varnish to the inside and outside of the basket.

TOOTHBRUSH HOLDER

Graphic and modern, this toothbrush holder is perfect for a tidy bathroom. The basketwork itself will need a neat approach too. Don't rush it!

INSTRUCTIONS

To give you a better view of some of the stages,
I have placed a white card inside the basketwork.

Base

1. Start with a round slath base (see page 12) with the
base sticks, and use the 1.5mm (¹⁄₁₆in) undyed cane to
weave the base. Sharpen the ends of all twenty-four
stakes to a point, and use a bodkin to insert them into
the base weave.

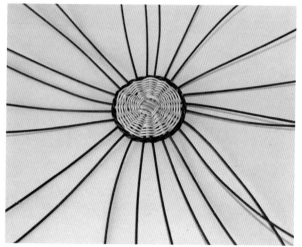

2. Weave an upsett using triple weave (see page 19)
with the three 35cm (13¾in) rods, and then prick up
the stakes.

Siding

3. Weave three rounds of pairing weave (see page 18)
with two rods of undyed cane. Start opposite the end
of the upsett weave. Then, space out three new rods
as shown and weave one round of three-rod slewing.

4. Insert the glass, and start to weave one violet cane so
that it begins one interval after the previous weave.

5. Make thirteen continuous rounds with violet randing and undyed cane slewing, as shown above. Complete the thirteenth round in violet by inserting it one interval after the end of the undyed cane.

6. Make three rounds of pairing weave with the two 1.5mm (¹⁄₁₆in) undyed weavers. Insert the end of each stake firmly back into the weave at its base to double each stake.

Border

7. Soak all the stakes and then cut each of the loops you have made. Start a trac border with the following pattern: in front of two stakes, behind one, in front of one.

Finishing

8. Leave to dry for twenty-four hours at room temperature, away from direct sunlight. Trim off any stubs (see page 25). Brush on a coat of waterproof varnish to the inside and outside of the work.

COTTON BALL BOX

Keep your cotton balls and cosmetic wipes tidy with this compact little woven box with separate lid.

MATERIALS

Base

- 6 base sticks 6.5cm (2½in) long in 4mm (¹¹⁄₆₄in) undyed cane
- 24 stakes 20cm (7¾in) long in 2mm (¹⁄₁₆in) black cane
- 3 rods 35cm (13¾in) long in 2mm (¹⁄₁₆in) black cane for the upsett

Siding

- Lengths of 1.5mm (¹⁄₁₆in) undyed and violet cane
- 1 straight glass 10cm (4in) high

Lid

- 12 stakes 30cm (11¾in) long in 2mm (¹⁄₁₆in) black cane
- 4 rods 30cm (11¾in) long in 1.5mm (¹⁄₁₆in) pink cane for the upsett
- Lengths of 1.5mm (¹⁄₁₆in) undyed cane

Size of the box: 8cm (3¼in) high.

INSTRUCTIONS

To make the base and the siding, follow the instructions for the toothbrush holder (see pages 120–123).

Lid

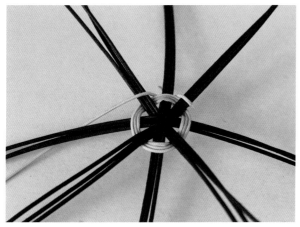

1. Find the middle of the four bunches of three black cane rods, and arrange them in a double cross (as shown). Start the weave using a single strand of 1.5mm (1/16in) undyed cane over and under each bunch, three rounds in one direction, and then three rounds back in the other (you can keep the spokes in place with a wire tie).

2. Make four rounds of pairing weave (see page 18) with two rods of 1.5mm (1/16in) undyed cane.

3. Weave a decorative band (see page 16) using the four 30cm (11¾in) rods in pink cane in a four-rod waling weave.

Border

4. Insert the end of each stake back into the pink weave at its base, forming a loop. Cut the loops to create a set of double stakes.

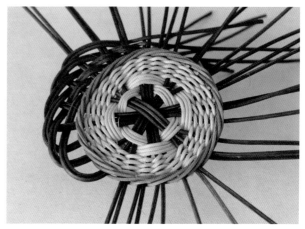

5. Bend down each pair of two stakes and make a trac border as follows: in front of two, behind one, in front of one, and finish behind.

Fitting the lid

6. On the back of the lid, cut off one of each pair of border stakes and then make two rounds of pairing weave (see page 18).

7. Finish by making a scallop border (see page 21).

Handle

8. Insert one doubled pink cane plus a single cane into the cross base (as shown), plait together for 4cm (1½in), and then insert the ends opposite to secure a plaited handle.

Finishing

9. Leave to dry for twenty-four hours at room temperature and away from direct sunlight. Trim off any stubs (see page 25). Brush on a coat of waterproof varnish to the inside and outside of the box.